# Health AND Fitness

# Healthy Food

A. R. Schaefer

Heinemann
LIBRARY

**www.heinemannlibrary.co.uk**
Visit our website to find out more information about Heinemann Library books.

**To order:**

☎ Phone +44 (0) 1865 888066

🖷 Fax +44 (0) 1865 314091

💻 Visit www.heinemannlibrary.co.uk

© Heinemann Library is an imprint of Capstone Global Library Limited, a company incorporated in England and Wales having its registered office at 7 Pilgrim Street, London, EC4V 6LB – Registered company number: 6695582

"Heinemann" is a registered trademark of Pearson Education Limited, under licence to Capstone Global Library Limited.

Text © Capstone Global Library Limited 2010
First published in hardback in 2010
The moral rights of the proprietor have been asserted.

Edited by Charlotte Guillain and Catherine Veitch
Designed by Kimberly R. Miracle and Betsy Wernert
Picture research by Elizabeth Alexander and Rebecca Sodergren
Production by Duncan Gilbert
Originated by Dot Gradations Ltd.
Printed in China by South China Printing Company Ltd.

ISBN 978 0 431015 31 6 (hardback)
14 13 12 11 10 09
10 9 8 7 6 5 4 3 2 1

**British Library Cataloguing in Publication Data**
Schaefer, Adam
Healthy food. - (Health and fitness)
613.2
A full catalogue record for this book is available from the British Library.

**Acknowledgements**

We would like to thank the following for permission to reproduce photographs: © Capstone Global Library Ltd. p. **12** (Tudor Photography); Alamy p. **16** (© Image Source Pink); Getty Images p. **6** (Altrendo Images); Photolibrary pp. **13** (Age Fotostock/Emilio Ereza), **19** (Rosenfeld), **20** (Foodfolio/ Imagestate), **22** (Image Source), **23** (Banana Stock), **24** (Fresh Food Images/Maximilian Stock Ltd.), **25** (Comstock/Dynamic Graphics), **27** (Mark Bolton/Garden Picture Library), **28** (James Darell/Digital Vision); Rex Features pp. **8** (Image Source), **29** (Deddeda/Design Pics Inc.); Science Photo Library p. **5** (Anthony Cooper); Shutterstock pp. **4** (© Galina Barskaya), **7** (© Elena Talberg), **10** (© debr22pics), **11** (© Geanina Bechea), **14** (© emily2k), **15** & **26** (© Kiselev Andrey Valerevich), **17** (© Monkey Business Images), **18** (© Janet Hastings), **21** (© R. Gino Santa Maria).

Cover photograph of a girl eating an apple reproduced with permission of PunchStock (Digital Vision).

The publishers would like to thank Nicole Clark for her assistance in the preparation of this book.

Every effort has been made to contact copyright holders of any material reproduced in this book. Any omissions will be rectified in subsequent printings if notice is given to the publisher.

All the Internet addresses (URLs) given in this book were valid at the time of going to press. However, due to the dynamic nature of the Internet, some addresses may have changed, or sites may have changed or ceased to exist since publication. While the author and Publishers regret any inconvenience this may cause readers, no such changes can be accepted by either the author or the Publishers.

# Contents

Some words are shown in bold, **like this**. You can find out what they mean by looking in the glossary.

# Healthy food

Sometimes people say that you are what you eat. The food you eat can make you healthy or unhealthy. It is your choice.

People who eat healthy food feel good.

Eating well is one part of a healthy life. We should all try to eat healthy food and try to have a **balanced diet**.

Vegetables are a type of healthy food.

# Eating regular meals

**Your choice:**

**Your choice:**

Do you think it is a good idea to eat one very big meal? Or is it better to eat several smaller meals during the day?

Eating the right amount of food is important.

It is better to eat smaller meals throughout the day. These meals give your body the **energy** it needs throughout the whole day.

A healthy sandwich will give you energy for hours.

# Balancing your diet

Everyone needs to eat a range of different food to stay healthy. **Wholegrain** bread is a healthy food. But eating only bread is not healthy.

Eat food from all of these food groups to stay healthy.

Each colour on this plate is for one of the five food groups.

Your **diet** is the food that you eat each day. **Protein**, **grains**, fruit and vegetables, milk, and fats are all important parts of a healthy diet.

# Healthy grains

**Your choice:**

A doughnut has a lot of flour in it. Flour is made from **grains**. Is eating a doughnut a good way to get grains in your **diet**?

A lot of people like doughnuts, but are they healthy?

10

Doughnuts are not a very healthy food. They are made with grains, but also with a lot of sugar and **fat**. Healthy grains include **wholegrain** bread and pasta, brown rice, and cereals.

Try to eat healthy grains a few times each day.

# Healthy fruit

Fruit contains **vitamins** that are healthy for you.

Fruit is great for your body. Fresh fruit is the best for your health. Fresh fruit has not been cooked and looks like it has just been picked.

Apples, oranges, bananas, pears, and berries all taste good fresh. Canned, dried, and frozen fruit is also healthy.

Food like fruit sweets, ice cream, and tarts should not be a part of a healthy **diet** each day.

# Healthy vegetables

**Your choice:**

You know vegetables are healthy. You can eat a fresh salad or chips. Which one is a better choice?

Chips are made from potatoes, but are they healthy?

Fresh vegetables are better for your health than **fried** food. A salad with fresh spinach, lettuce, tomatoes, and other vegetables is very healthy. Cooked vegetables, like carrots, baked potatoes, and broccoli are also healthy.

Eat uncooked vegetables to get the most **nutrients**.

# Healthy milk food

Milk food is an important part of a good **diet**. Yogurt and cheese are made from milk. This food helps your bones grow strong.

Dairy products like these are good for your teeth and bones.

There is cheese on these nachos, but it is not a very healthy meal.

Yogurt and milk are healthy dairy food. A little cheese and butter is fine, but you should not eat too much as they contain a lot of **fat**. Ice cream is a dairy food but has too much fat and sugar to be healthy every day.

# Healthy proteins

## Your choice:

There is **protein** in chicken.
Is **fried** chicken a healthy
way to eat protein?

Meats like chicken
contain a lot of protein.

Fried food is mostly unhealthy. Small amounts of **grilled** meat, chicken, and fish are much healthier. There is also a lot of healthy protein in nuts and beans.

Protein helps build muscles in your body.

# Fats

Healthy fats are an important part of our diet.

**Fats** help keep our skin and other **organs** healthy. But some fats are healthier choices than others. Healthy fats come from fruit, nuts, and vegetables, such as avocados.

Try to limit the food you eat that is high in **animal fat**, such as beefburgers and **fried** meat. This food is full of unhealthy fats.

Most fast food is high in unhealthy fats.

# Water and other liquids

**Your choice:**

We know that we need to drink water to live. Fizzy drinks are mostly water. Are fizzy drinks a good way to drink water?

Avoid drinks with a lot of sugar and chemicals.

Drink several glasses of water each day.

While fizzy drinks have water in them, other ingredients make these drinks unhealthy, such as sugar. The best drink is plain water. Fruit juice is nice to drink with meals but it also contains a lot of sugar so it is best not to drink too much.

# Unhealthy food

**Your choice:**

Some food, such as beefburgers
and ice cream, is bad for our health.
Should we never eat those things?

Do not eat too much food
with lots of sugar and fat.

Eating unhealthy food, such as cakes, biscuits, and crisps does not help our bodies to grow and stay well. But if we eat healthy food most of the time, an occasional treat is alright and can be fun.

A little ice cream or chocolate is fine at a special time, such as a birthday party.

# Fresh food is fantastic

For most food, fresh is best. Fresh fruit and vegetables have more **nutrients** in them than food that has been kept in plastic packets or cans.

Fresh fruit looks good, too.

Mouldy or bad-smelling food is not good for us and can make us ill. It is a good idea to check bread and cheese for **mould**. Make sure that fruit and vegetables are firm and ripe.

Mouldy food can make you ill.
It smells and looks unhealthy.

# Healthy habits for life

It is easier to get into good eating **habits** when you are around other people who have good habits. Ask your family and friends to start eating healthily with you.

A meal or snack always tastes better when you share it.

Healthy habits can last your whole life.

It is never too late or too early to start eating well. Even people who have been unhealthy for years feel better when they start to eat well. Getting into good habits while you are young will start a lifetime of healthy eating.

# Glossary

**animal fat** part of an animal that is not very healthy for humans to eat

**balanced diet** diet that has a mix of different foods. Includes proteins, grains, vegetables, fruit, fats, and milk.

**diet** what you usually eat and drink

**energy** power needed for your body to work and stay alive

**fat** oil found in some food

**fried** cooked in oil or another fat

**grain** seed from a cereal plant, such as wheat or maize

**grill** cook food by putting it close to something hot

**habit** thing you do often

**mould** kind of organism that grows on rotten things

**nutrient** substance (such as a vitamin or protein) that people need to grow and stay healthy

**organ** part inside your body that does certain jobs

**protein** part of some food that helps the body to grow and stay healthy

**vitamin** part of some food that helps the body to grow and stay healthy

**wholegrain** grain such as oats, wheat, corn, or rice that have all or most of their natural fibre and nutrients

# Find out more

## Books to read

*All Kinds of Drinks (Healthy Eating)*, Susan Martineau (Franklin Watts, 2006)

*Food Groups*, Lola Schaefer (Heinemann Library, 2009)

*Go Facts: Healthy Eating*, Paul McEvoy (A & C Black, 2005)

*Healthy Eating (Health Choices)*, Cath Senker (Wayland, 2007)

*What's on Your Plate?*, Ted and Lola Schaefer (Raintree, 2006)

## Websites

www.5aday.nhs.uk
Click on "Fun & Games" and then "Did You Know?" to find out some amazing food facts.

www.eatwell.gov.uk/healthydiet/eatwellplate/
This website teaches you how to eat a balanced diet, by using the eatwell plate.

www.nutrition.org.uk
Find some great recipe ideas here, by clicking on "cook club".

# Index

balanced diet 5, 8–9, 30
beans 19
bones 16
bread 8, 11, 27

cheese 16, 17, 27
chicken 18, 19

dairy food 16–17

energy 7, 30

fats 9, 11, 17, 20–21, 24,
    30
fizzy drinks 22, 23
food groups 8–9
fresh food 12, 13, 15, 26
fried food 14, 15, 18, 19,
    21, 30
fruit and fruit juices 9,
    12–13, 20, 23, 26, 27

grains 8, 9, 10, 11, 30

healthy habits 28–29, 30

ice cream 13, 17, 24, 25

meat 18, 19, 21
milk 9, 16, 17

mouldy food 27, 30
muscles 19

nutrients 15, 26, 30
nuts 19, 20

pasta 11
protein 9, 18–19, 30

regular meals 6–7
rice 11

salads 15
sandwiches 7
smaller meals 6, 7
sugar 11, 17, 22, 23, 24
sweets 13

teeth 16

unhealthy food 24–25

vegetables 5, 9, 14–15,
    20, 26, 27
vitamins 12, 30

water 22, 23
wholegrain food 8, 11, 30

yogurt 16, 17